LOOK AT ME!
I CAN PAINT

By Sarah Hewetson
Illustrated by Kate Simpson and Keith Newell

a Joshua Morris book
from The Reader's Digest Association, Inc.

With special thanks to: Daniel, age 6; Thomas, age 6; Edward, age 4;
Thomas, age 6; and Sam, age 6, for their help in testing the activities.

A Joshua Morris Book
Published by The Reader's Digest Association, Inc.
Printed in China
ISBN: 0-89577-598-0
2 4 6 8 10 9 7 5 3 1

Contents

	Page
Things You'll Need	4
Make Your Own Brushes	5
Make Your Own Paints	6
Mixing Colors	8
Lots of Dots	10
Straw Splatters	12
Seeing Double	14
Silly String	16
Marble Magic	18
It's a Secret	20
Print-a-Pattern	22
The Ultimate Self-Portrait	24
Cut and Paint	26
Wacky Wax	28
Paint Mix-Ins	30
Art Show	32

Note to parents:
Children love to paint, but they will need some
help. Please supervise the use of paint, scissors,
and glue so that your child will enjoy
a safe and rewarding learning experience.

Things You'll Need

You probably already have most of the art materials needed for the activities in this book, but if not, they're all readily available at art, hobby, or toy stores. You should be able to find the other items you'll need around your house.

Poster Paint
Poster paint comes ready-mixed or as a powder that you mix with water. It is a thick paint.

Watercolor Paint
This comes in small blocks of color that you wet. It is a thin paint.

Paintbrushes
Thin brushes work best with watercolor paints, fat brushes with poster paints.

Paper
White drawing paper or colored construction paper will work for most of the projects in this book. You can use old boxes when cardboard is needed for a project.

Look for these special symbols. They serve as a guide to how difficult an activity is:

quick and easy

takes some time

your child may need extra help

4

Make Your Own Brushes

Even if you have a wide variety of paintbrushes, you'll want to try some of these adventurous ideas for making your own brushes! By using some surprising items from around the house or outdoors, you can give your pictures all kinds of interesting looks!

Cotton-Ball Brush
Glue a cotton ball onto the end of a twig or pencil.

Straw Brush
Tie or tape a small handful of straw, hay, or grass onto a twig or pencil.

Feather Brush
Use feathers from a household feather duster or birds' feathers tied or taped onto a twig or pencil. Or just use a single feather on its own.

Vegetable Brush
Try using a carrot top or the floweret end of broccoli or cauliflower as a paintbrush!

Make Your Own Paints

Long ago, before there were art stores, artists had to make their own paints. Why don't you try creating your own paints the same way that they did?

You will need:

- **Colored chalk** ▪ **Small bags** ▪ **A rolling pin**
▪ **Blueberries, strawberries, or raspberries** ▪ **1 or 2 cups**
▪ **A spoon** ▪ **2 eggs** ▪ **A bowl** ▪ **A few small containers**

Step 1
Put each color of chalk into a separate bag and crush it into dust with a rolling pin. Mush the berries in separate cups with a spoon.

Step 2
Crack the eggs into the bowl and pour off the egg whites, keeping the yolks in the bowl.

Step 4
Add a different crushed chalk or berry to each container and mix it in.

Step 3
Add a drop of water to the egg yolks and stir until smooth. Divide the mixture among the small containers.

Try using catsup, mustard, or fruit juice as paint! Your creations will look delicious!

7

Mixing Colors

Even if you have just a few colors of paint, you can make more. By mixing your paints, you can make new colors that will add variety to your paintings.

Use a plate as your mixing palette. Dip your brush in one color and put the paint on the plate. Rinse your brush thoroughly and then dip it in another color. Mix it into the paint already on the plate. You've created another color!

All you need to start with are red, yellow, and blue.

 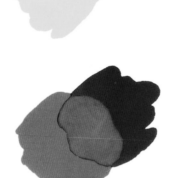 

Red and yellow make orange

Red and blue make purple

Yellow and blue make green

Once you have made these colors, you can use them to make more!

Blue and green make turquoise

Red and green make brown

If you have white paint, you can mix it with all your bright colors to make paler shades. The more white you add, the paler the color becomes.

Don't be afraid to use bright colors together — even red with hot pink. Bright combinations will give your paintings a zingy look.

A light color looks bright on a dark background.

Lots of Dots

Put your paintbrushes away for this activity and use cotton swabs instead! Creating pictures with dots gives your work a very different look. So dot away!

You will need:

- **Sheets of white drawing or colored construction paper** ▪ **A pencil**
- ▪ **Poster paints** ▪ **Cotton swabs**

Step 1
Use a pencil very lightly to draw your picture on a piece of paper.

Step 2
Dip a swab in paint. Make an outline of dots around the main shapes. Use a new swab for each color.

Step 3
Fill in the shapes with lots of dots. Then add dots of accent colors. To make smaller dots, pull the cotton off the swab and use the end of the stick.

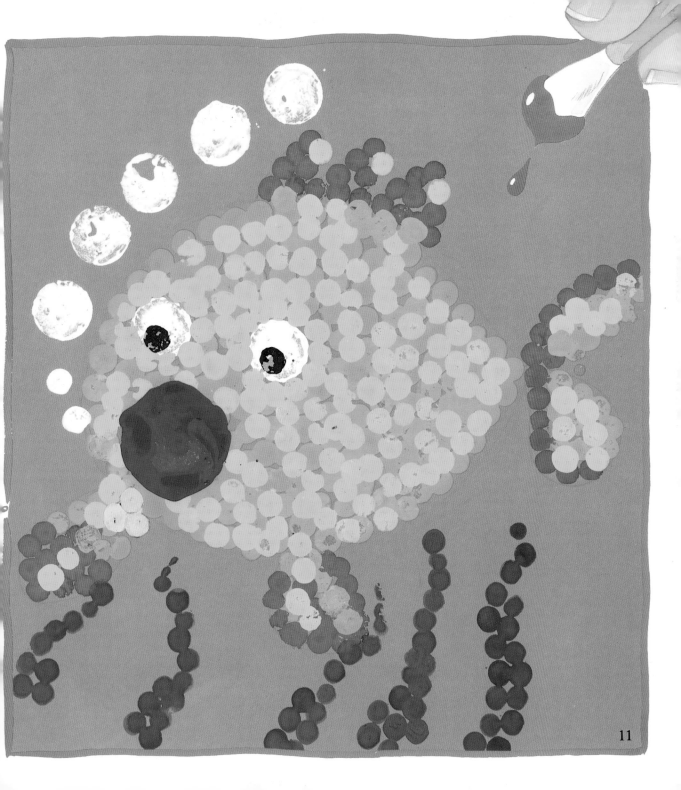

Try tearing colored paper into pieces and glue them onto your design. Make a rocket with a colorful trail or a bursting star.

Straw Splatters

You can make some weird and wacky paintings using drinking straws.
So take a deep breath and get ready to paint!

You will need:

- **Sheets of white drawing or colored construction paper**
- **Poster paints**
- **A paintbrush**
- **Drinking straws**

Step 1
Mix your poster paints with enough water so that they are runny.

Step 2
Drip some paint onto a piece of paper with a paintbrush or paint a few lines.

Step 3
Use a straw to blow the paint across the paper. Add more colors to the paper and mix them as you blow.

> Your splattered designs can be more than artwork — use them as wrapping papers.

Seeing Double

Here's a way to "double the fun" of painting. You can paint only half a picture and make a whole one, like this butterfly. Or make twin pictures — battling dinosaurs, for example.

You will need:
- **Sheets of white drawing or colored construction paper**
- **Poster paints**
- **Thick paintbrushes**

Step 1
Fold your piece of paper in half and then smooth it out so that it lies flat.

Step 2

Paint your picture on one half of the folded sheet, making sure you don't paint across the fold line.

Step 3

While the paint is still wet, fold the paper in half and press down evenly. Carefully open the paper.

If you've made a wacky print, wait for your picture to dry, then cut it into the shape of whatever you think it looks like!

15

Silly String

This activity uses the same folding method as SEEING DOUBLE, but with a twist. By putting string dipped in paint between the folded paper, you can make some swirly, whirly pictures!

You will need:

- **Sheets of white drawing or colored construction paper**
- **Poster paints**
- **A few small containers**
- **String, cut into lengths 2–3 inches (5–8 cm) longer than the width of the paper**
- **A spoon or stick to stir with**

Step 1
Fold your piece of paper in half and then smooth it out so that it lies flat again.

Step 2
Put a different paint color into each container. Stir one or more pieces of string into each color.

Step 3
Twist and twirl each piece of string onto one half of the paper. Make sure both ends of each string stick out over the edge.

Use smooth packing string, fuzzy yarn, and scratchy twine for some fun effects!

Step 4
Fold the paper in half over the string. Hold down the paper with one hand and pull out each string with the other hand. Carefully open the paper.

Marble Magic

Try shooting your marbles around in paint rather than on the sidewalk. Don't forget to wash the marbles off when you're done!

You will need:

- **Sheets of white drawing or colored construction paper**
- **A shallow box lid**
- **Tape**
- **Poster paints**
- **A few small containers**
- **Marbles**
- **A spoon**

Step 1
Tape a piece of paper into the box lid.

Step 2
Put a different paint color into each container. Drop 2 or 3 marbles into each container. Lift them out with the spoon and put them in the lid.

Step 3
Tilt the lid so that the marbles roll all over the paper. When the paint on the marbles is used up, put them back into the containers and roll again!

Cut your marble designs into different shapes and paste them onto colored paper. Try colorful fish in a blue sea or flowers on a green lawn.

It's a Secret

Your paints can be used like invisible ink. Your message or drawing is only revealed after you put the paint on the paper.

You will need:
- **Sheets of white drawing paper**
- **A white crayon**
- **Watercolor paints**
- **A paintbrush**

Step 1
Using the crayon, draw a secret treasure map or a spooky picture on a sheet of paper.

Step 2
Paint over your drawing with the watercolor paints. Use any colors you like. The paint won't cover the wax crayon, so your drawing is revealed.

Draw or write a message to your friends and then let them do the painting to see what you've said!

Print-a-Pattern

Use items from around your house and yard to make animals, scenes, or fun prints.

You will need:
- **Sheets of drawing paper**
- **Paper plates**
- **Poster paints**
- **A fat paintbrush**
- **Leaves, sponge shapes, and orange halves**

Step 1
On separate plates, mix each color with a little water. Press the shape you want to print into the thick paint.

Step 2
Lay the painted shape face down on the paper. Press down gently with your fingers. Carefully lift the shape away from the paper.

Try using a bottle cap, cork, or sliced vegetables. Experiment with as many different things as you like!

23

The Ultimate Self-Portrait

This activity shows you how to create the best picture of all — a portrait of yourself! You'll need a friend to help you, and you'll need to do it where there's a lot of space to spread out!

You will need:
- **Sheets of white construction paper**
- **Tape**
- **A crayon**
- **Poster paints**
- **A paintbrush**

Try painting yourself in fancy clothes or as a clown, a pirate, or a dancer.

Step 1
Tape the sheets of paper together. Make the paper area big enough so that you can lie down on it. All the edges need to be taped down.

Step 2
Turn the paper over so that the tape is on the back. Lie down on the paper and ask your friend to trace around you on the paper with the crayon.

Step 3
Paint the figure so that it looks like you — as you are or a "pretend" you.

24

Cut and Paint

You can mix painting with photographs to create some extra-special pictures. Ask permission before you cut up the magazines, and have someone older help you cut them up.

You will need: ▪ **Old magazines** ▪ **Scissors** ▪ **Sheets of white drawing paper** ▪ **Glue** ▪ **A pencil** ▪ **Poster paints** ▪ **A paintbrush**

Step 1
Cut out photos from old magazines. Then cut out the portions that you want to use in your painting.

Step 2
Arrange the magazine cuttings on the paper and glue them in place. With a pencil, lightly join the pieces together with the outlines of your drawing.

Step 3
Use poster paints to color in the areas you've drawn.

Photos of people, animals, vehicles, and background scenery work well with this project.

27

Wacky Wax

Wax crayons are waterproof and don't mix with paint. But you can create some wonderful pictures using them together in this special way.

You will need:
- **Sheets of white drawing paper**
  - **Crayons**
  - **Black poster paint**
    - **A paintbrush**
    - **A spoon**

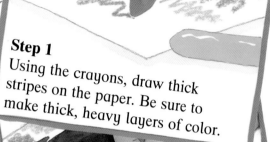

Step 1
Using the crayons, draw thick stripes on the paper. Be sure to make thick, heavy layers of color.

Step 2
Paint over the stripes of crayon with black poster paint. Make sure all the stripes are completely covered. Let the paint dry.

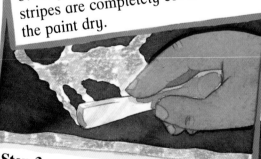

Step 3
Using the end of a spoon, scratch through the paint to make your picture. Be careful not to scratch through the crayon underneath.

Paint Mix-Ins

You can give your poster paints different textures if you mix them with certain ingredients. Using these kinds of paints will add texture and a 3-D effect to your creations.

You will need:
- **Thick drawing paper or cardboard**
- **Poster paints**
- **A few small containers**
- **Clean, dry sand or crushed breakfast cereal**
- **A few plastic spoons**
- **Paintbrushes**

Don't make the mixtures too thick or they won't stick to your paintbrushes.

Step 1
Put some poster paint into each small container. Mix some of the sand or cereal into the paint.

Step 2
Paint a picture of whatever you'd like and build up the thickness of the paint as you go along.

Art Show

Now that you are an artist, why not show off your paintings? Ask if you can have an art show. Turn the garage or a room in the house into your own art gallery, and invite your family and friends to come and take a look.

You can put your pictures on cardboard or on larger pieces of paper and paint frames to go around them. Frames will really show off your paintings!

Some of your paintings will make great birthday cards or note paper. You can cut them into a card size and fold them, or fold the entire painting and write on the back of it.